HARRIET WILLIAMS

Stepping out of your shell

Dedicated to all victims of self hate, low self esteem, victims of derogatory speeches, shamed physically and emotionally. Victims of suicide, that one that thinks he has to please the world to belong.

You are amazingly beautiful, like yours smiles twinkles like stars, the maker never makes mistake in his art.
Dedicated as well to all bullies out there, aren't you tired of the mocking sentence, is that how jobless you can be.

Dedicated to the maker.

Contents

1.

2.

1.

3.

4.
   1.
 2.
   3.
   4.
5.
 1.
   2.
6.
 1.
7.
 1.
   2.
   3.
8.
9.

Preface

Do you have the sensation of being worthless, comparison with anyone around you, the lack of self confidence, feelings of not matching up to standards, uncertainty about yourself, the need to stay away from individuals, avoiding responsibilities, consistently fretted over others opinion in regards to you.

Or is it the problem of body shaming, we are often called derogatory terms regarding our weight — it could be anything from fat, obese, anorexic, flabby or skinny. The negativity swirling around, overwhelming our self confidence, are you in this phase.

The initials are Harriet Williams, introducing you to a concise story, it could be mistaken for a high school novel, and it likewise be mistaken for a counseling book.

This is a story depicting the struggles, the insecurities youthful grown up, youngsters face, and is a reminder to them that the could step out of the shackles bounding them.

The low self-esteem depressed victim, reminder to them, that they are God's art piece made with the purest canvas. Beauty isn't just characterized with the outward look, excellence is your personality, your confidence, your worth, everything revolving you.

Most cases, teenagers finds it a bit difficult confiding and let know of their torment to their guardians, until the storms gets too heavy to handle, the feeling of know one understands, because you think, the bearer of the shoe knows where the pain is located at, insinuating (you are not in my place, so quit acting like you care).

This sentence has been heard, by many guardians, sincerely am not in your place, but rather I have seen my own portion of unfairness, the inclination that life sucks, I comprehend that quite alright, however it doesn't make any difference, what is important is the way am responding to life, same with you.

Gratitude for beginning this journey with me.

One

A new phase

Lisa hurry up is your first day in college mom's voice sounded once again. Grunted out in frustration, at the intrusion to my beautiful sleep, was supposed to be beaming in happiness, starting off a new chapter, which is college, but I couldn't help but feel more depressed.

Hello everyone my initials are Lisa Esteban presently eighteen, today is my alleged first day of resumption in Avac medical college. College worth profound respect and excitement, still my mood, could contend with the sourness of a lime.(intention: sarcastic). Stretching out my hands to the counter beside my bed stand, in search of my glasses, Lisa !!!!!!! Mum yelled, once more. Gosh my earbuds are bleeding, getting up already countered back. Hauling my lazy feet up after minutes of silence, with a blank mind, moved my lazy ass to the mirror situated not far from my bed. The haziness of the room, made it difficult to make due of the time.

3

A girl with scattered and messy curls, gazed back at me, her green eyes held mine, the tiny freckles scattered beneath her eyes glittered in alignment with the light. The round glasses giving her a nerd look complimented her appearance in an awkward manner. I loathed my appearance, being taunted with snide remarks, although mother's words were an opposite version. The fact that she regards me as the most beautiful girl, says it all.

Her words were merely fallacies and exaggerations to make me feel elated. My eyebrows jerked disapprovingly. Obviously you can regard me as the girl that hid behind everyone, in evasion of too much attention, the individual that wants to contribute to a conversation but not certain about herself.

The girl that mostly is acquainted with the ground rather to human faces, not that she cherishes it that way, but doesn't have enough boldness to stare at faces when engaged in conversation, her words are somewhat hurried, when facing an opposite gender, in fear that her looks are minor, comparing anyone her sight fixes on, depressed all night, about a thousand things wrong with her features, turning down invitation, because she doesn't believe she's worth it. Your typical introvert, my inferiority complex were of top notch. Took a glance once again at myself.

Sluggishly, knelt down and prayed to God for a blessed first day in school. Dragged my unwilling feet to the lavatory to run a shower. Envisioning mother's face overflowing with allot of lectures, which I wasn't really in the mood to listen to, a smile found its way to my lips.

After God knows how long, decided to leave the solace of my shower and face reality. Speaking about reality, am this perfect extrovert, created in my illusions and imaginations, however the harsh whip of reality made my eyes open painfully. Have you at any point felt this feeling, of being an astonishing character in your dream, but when those beautiful eyes, face reality you discover you are just less of your fantasies.

Wanted something beautiful for my first day, we weren't well off but we were fairly okay. Mother owns a local bookstore few blocks away from here. Life literally revolved around mother and I, ever since death has its clutches on dad. The only thing that am grateful in life, is the kind of lady figure i was bestowed with, my primary needs were always taken care of.

After a long racking of brain, and disorganizing my closet, settled on a tight jeans, with a crop top that is the same length with the waistline, pairing it up with a pair of black sneakers and a backpack, took my necessary stuff and the bag which mum packed in my belongings after she did a long cross check, went down for breakfast.

Similar eyes stared back at me, her straight shining black hair were rolled up in a bun, age had no effect on her effortless beauty and elegance. Truthfully speaking, been jealous of mum unexplained beauty, I don't know if you think is weird, but literally everyday, always make comparison between we both, most times it get crazy and I pray to wake up in her body, when she was a young adult, approximately my age, that's how deranged I could be.

Young lady, I guess am avac medical college billboard, her sarcastic words broke my thoughts, which were going overboard.

Chuckling dryly, rolled my eyes on her speech, just admiring God's piece of art, isn't too much to ask for, smirked playfully at her flushed face.

The prospect of leaving mum for the city, was unsettling, I don't Know how I will cope without her love and support, mingling with others, wasn't something I was keen on, my introverted self made things end on a bad note. The negative feeling swirling around, that others were better than me, that I wasn't enough, I can't do it, made me crawling back to my shell. Taking my breakfast, and listening to barrage of advices, we decided to start with our journey.

Been thirty minutes, since we left our abode, in the quest of, getting me settled in college, mum drove in silence, while I opted for a low rhythm track, to dwell in my thoughts.

Could feel the intense stare, drilling holes on my side face, what's it, broke the awkward atmosphere, glancing at mother's side features, could see stifled tears. What's going on, stared curiously for an answer, seeing her tears pricked my curiosity in an anxious manner.

little angel is grown, mom's words triggered my nervousness, in as much I acted unaffected, with the fact that am moving away, the unsettling knot gnawed at me heavily. Unrestrained tears escaped it's way through my eyes.

My love, you are the most amazing gift, nature blessed me with, mother voice shattered my walls, in which I built, never allow anyone step on you, tolerance has it boundaries, she continued her words, when it crosses the line, speak. Never knew mother was aware, of my inner battles. Did my best not to bother her, on whatsoever occurring in my life, with excuses I can handle it, but honestly was frightened of letting her know of my scars, was terrified will meet a disappointed gaze, well scared she will stare at me like a patient always in need of help.

Will miss you my baby, her voice drew me back to the present, stay clear off bad companies her other free hand, stretched forward to wipe away remnants of tears on my cheeks I will mother, assured her, conveying my emotions through my eyes. She stared at me briefly and smiled, the car's movement slowly came to an abrupt halt, lost in the moment, time moved ahead. We are already here, her sadness clearly reflected on her words. Her features softened with a longing gaze, it makes leaving scary.

The nervousness returned back, staring out of the window, could see the strong billboard with bold writings of "welcome to Avac medical college". My three years of medical course and three years of my life will be spent here, exhaled tiredly and nervously.

Young lady, time isn't a leisure for us, you have spent hours, delaying at home, let's get you inside, her mood did a 360 degree change. Wonder how she does that, muttered to myself, it makes wonder if the initial moment ever happened or it was all a cosplay.

Stepping out of the car the sunlight had it's delight on setting it's rays on my face. Mum had already, dragged my bag along with her, waiting for my feet to move accordance to hers.

Moving to her side, my eyes scanning around towards it's environment and taking in information, beautiful girls of the same age with me could be seen, moving around and chattering away happily, The guys weren't left behind, couldn't help but compare myself with them, couldn't help but think they were better, Or I might not stand a chance getting asked out by the guys. Which was actually a weird thought, Could feel my inner demons whispering deep into my soul, if only your hair was straight, if only your curls are arranged beautiful and not in a messy way, which takes you forever to smoothed, Making you always roll it in an awkward manner, if only your freckles weren't so visible,

Can you see, they way their all blabbing ceaselessly, dare you to last in a conversation, Never will you make friends with such ease, you are utterly delusional, thinking you are amazing, the whispers clawed it fingers, on my bleeding heart.

Your are too skinny, others have appropriate shape, it felt overwhelming, and the only redemption was for me, to avoid the gazes been thrown at me, to acquaint myself with the smooth titled surface of the surrounding.

Lisa watch out! mum suddenly shouted, being so lost and occupied with my thoughts, collided into someone, my face nested on her flowering layered gown, her fragrance assaulted my nostrils, such beautiful scent like lavender with a touch of rose. I caused a drama on my first day, could the day get worst, sighed at my clumsiness.

Worried and concerned voices, seeking to know, our well being, were heard above us, the thought to meet those criticizing looks made me slightly anxious. Thought of fainting came knocking to my brain.

Her voice severed off every strand of thought, left in me, please would you stand, my knees are scraped. Lifting my eyes her blue iris stared at mine irritated. Am sorry, fidgeted with my hands, mum surged in checking for any visible injuries, her worried gaze scanned every inch and crook of my skin.

I told you to be careful, you will definitely be the death of me, her complains filled my ears. Am so sorry, mum apologized to the other party, apologizing to them down-rightly felt right, but the feeling of bashfulness and anxiety made it far-fetched.

Isn't a big deal, anyways, ask your daughter to stick to the road, and not carelessly absentminded of her surroundings, her eyes twitched in a belittling way, her features similar with the black haired girl, a dumb, can easily foretell, the were indeed blood.

Glancing towards mum, could detect the rage about to seep out, how could one be shamelessly rude, muttered to myself, was enraged by her audaciousness, seconds turned to minutes, the dilating of mother's pupil, the curved arc of her eyebrows, the gritting sound of her teeth indicating war.

Mum, before I could finish my sentence, the Black haired girl interrupted my speech. Pardon my mother, she's quite overprotective, wasn't also paying attention, so I guess we were both clumsy, apologies for my tardiness, am Anastasia by the way, if you my excuse us, she ended her speech so fluently.

Elegance dripped all around her, her graceful and coordinated steps, together with her mother's haughty disposition graced my eyes, tilting my neck towards mother, could see her annoyed gestures, urging me to move ahead, no more dramatic moment.

Roselle's P.o.v.

Hours had been ticking away, my alleged new mate ought to have shown up. My name is Roselle, your typical obese kid, with a BMI of 29.9, which was considerably fat. Coming to avac medical college, one of the most popular colleges, accessible for various countries, gender, ethnicity, and coming all the way from Istanbul, living here with no family and with a new kid. That will join in with the sarcastic train, to probably make college life miserable than the hell my life was entangled with, ate me up quickly.

Fidgeting with my hands, and pacing around, a habit which I was accustomed with, when nervous. A knock made my hairs standing, is just another girl like you, breath in, chanted to myself once again, recollecting my nerves, stood up to get the door, but the knob twitched slightly, opening swiftly, my hazel eyes held those beautiful green ones.

Beautiful freckles scattered beneath her eyes contrasting with her pale skin, her green eyes gleamed like the lustrous glow of the forest. her messy curls dangled here and there, framing her oval face, she was an exquisite beauty, with the perfect shape, not fat and not too skinny.

Jealousy was a feeling I was accustomed to, although I don't let my demons control me, I love me, but I couldn't help but feel the pain, am only human and am embedded with emotions, staring at her, questioned the maker again, why the unfairness, tried everything but nothing worked, ate less, exercised, nothing helped, the doctors said it was genetic, masking my emotions, smiled at the stranger.

Hello, extended my greetings, the glasses gave her a smarty look, the name is Roselle, speculating you are my new mate, started at her for answers, sorry for intruding to your personal space, I blurted out after minutes of waiting for her to speak, cause obviously she literally wasn't speaking to me, think she's a snob, probably doesn't want anything to do with a fat kid.

Author remark: This reminds of a beautiful poet "A man's poison could be someone's delicacy"

Two

Friendship

Finally done with the registration, which took eternity to accomplish (being sarcastic). Block B room 12, stared at the door in front of me, with mixed emotions, don't know what type of individual, lies at the other edge. Rehearsed on my greetings, for strength, the thought of turning back, crossed me. Finally after much contemplation and weird stares from onlookers.

Decided to knock, turning the door knobs mistakenly, due to my clumsiness, it swiftly opened, leaving no room for options, but to let my presence known. Stared at the cute plump girl. her features which strikes an amazing comparison with an infant, made me nod in astonishment. Her hazel eyes twitched in innocence. Lost in my observation, which was a bit rude, my consciousness, wasn't paying attention to her words, until her last statement, hauled my reasoning back.

I might have left an impression of being a douche-bag, did it again chided myself, making everyone around me feel awkward. Am Lisa Esteban, you are right, am your new mate, let's get to make beautiful memories together, tried sounding polite and friendly, to repair the broken atmosphere. Couldn't survive if the one am sleeping with for the next three years becomes an enemy with me, due to my mix ups.

Her smiles and nod, calmed my guilty heart. Staring at my surroundings, the both beds were arranged in an opposite directions, beside each bed a wardrobe and a counter stood proudly, sighting the little door that leads to the lavatory, nodded in satisfaction.

Finally here breathed out, wanted to strike a conversation with her, kept formulating words to speak and how to present them, making the room awfully quiet, and my first impression really left me hanging on a thin rope.

Before the words could breathe out freely from my mouth, her friendly voice beats me to it. So is the first time staying away from home her eyes curious on me, I appreciated the little talks, it made me feel wanted and moreover the silence was nerve racking.

Yes answered her with smiles, will miss home especially mum, we both talked about few other things, her family and so on, the bonding really got me surprised, never bonded or spoke so casual with anyone, if not family, leading me to paint some untruths, just for her to not be bored of me, cause it felt like a dream.

Minutes turned to hours, fully settled, we decided to explore the surroundings, today was the deadline for resident student to get settled in their designated rooms. Avac medical college is much bigger than the rumors whispered to the company beside me, could see her amused face, yes she whispered back, making me chuckle, why are we whispering muttered loudly, same question on my mind, she giggled in a childlike manner.

Making me shift my attention towards her, her features were indeed like that of a new born baby. Her round eyes similar to Mrs. Charlotte baby, that lives few blocks away from my abode. Shook my head slightly, focused my attention, to the matter on hand, don't want to cause another drama.

Towards the laboratory, allot of facilities were seen, they live up to their name, Roselle muttered beside me, I nodded in admiration, could see probably our senior colleagues, all on full lab attire attending to something with an abrupt attention, which caught my interest. They seem to sight out presence, making us scurry away, to another section, which was the canteen, foods were on display, the neatness and diligence, fueled my respect more.

Exploring different medical sections and blocks, tiredness crept in. Bringing our little adventure to a halt. Trudging back towards our room, Roselle's tapping, made me grunt out in frustration, not now, the bed is calling me, retorted back lazily, take a look first, her voice urged me silently, stared at her questioningly, common not me, there, her eye traced a figure. Glancing towards the direction, unwillingly,

Wow!! that was my first expression, a work of God's art stood in front of us, her Afro so thick and beautiful, her brownish eye staring at the onlookers, could see the stares were getting to her, her complexion was as dark as nightfall. Haven't seen anyone as dark as she was, seen a lot of blacks, but hers were rare.

Some group of hot arrogant looking guys passed towards her, while leaving a snide comment, "damn girl wonder if you stain others" which made their lackey's to burst out in laughter, could see her glossy eyes, tears were threatening to blink out, my introverted self didn't want much attention to me. In spite of the fury burning within me, I wasn't powerless, but I couldn't bring myself to assist her, to ask her if she's alright,

Until I felt Roselle's pull towards the dark goddess. Her eyes stared to us, and one thing I could read in those earthy colored orbs(eyes) were the pleading to take her away from there, how could people be so cruel, murdering someone isn't when a trigger is pulled and the slugs are let loose on a human skull. Words are actually the fastest way to do that.

Casual jokes to make everyone laugh, remarks on a person characteristics in awful manner all in terms of it was a harmless humor. While you send such person to a depreciating state and more into their shell. Knew exactly her torment cause I have been there.

They must be visually impaired not to acknowledge your beauty, Roselle voice and friendly tone did the trick, her Barbie looking face pulled up in smiles. Roselle wasn't really uttering those words to make her feel elated, The were indeed delusive, not to acknowledge her beauty. Not exaggerating but, the girl in front of me was really a rare exquisite beauty, her honeyed earthy colored eyes danced in alignment with diamonds. Her face carved in a doll like manner, gave her the features of a goddess, the perfect shape to accentuate her beauty.

Height so perfect, Aphrodite has indeed seen, her competitor. You are really rare and so beautiful, told her from the deepest part of my reasoning, not letting my bashfulness getting in the way, relayed my thoughts to her.

Her smiles looked blinding, sincerely appreciate your kindness, call me Felicia Donald, her voice as perfect as her looks, The Maker really outdid his creation, after our brief introduction, and finding out her room number and what course she was opting for, which coincidentally matched with ours made the day more amazing

Three

Indeed lessons

The buzzing sound of the alarm woke me from my drowsiness, it's orientation day, fluttering my eyes open, stared at the ceiling, for quite a while, am really in college and I wasn't dreaming, it really was reality muttered to myself, made two amazing friends, to others might not be an accomplishment, or thing worth celebrating, but to an introvert like me, it really was a great deal. Tilting my neck to the other side, could see Roselle sleeping face, felt bad waking her up, but Today is orientation day, we shouldn't miss out.

………..,,,,,,,,,,,,,,,,………

Felicia's p.o.v

Hello Mama have settled in and I made two new cool friends, my complexion was really cherished, just like you predicted, the outcome of things, came out unexpectedly great. A beautiful girl called me a rare beauty, sincerity laced in her words, they really weren't faking it, it was genuine this Time mama, and am so happy, today is orientation day, have to get ready, talk when am back, love you Mama send greetings to papa and the press button was turned on by my thumb.

My name is Felicia Donald, earlier on I made a quick introduction, but let me bring you in my story. Black is beautiful they say and is not questionable, but my darkness was recorded as the blackest in most places of the world. Hailing from the northern part of Africa, being dark could be explained, but my extreme melanin couldn't. Being taunted, used as instances, for examples, being just eighteen, life has really shown me, it's unfairness.

Yesterday thought me a better one, I was indeed rare, Lisa words really touched my soul, my beauty was God's definition of art and I won't let myself sulk over words, questions, had been tossed at me, do I stain others, the pain which I felt, when I heard that was indeed, unfathomable.

Never joked with my personal hygiene, my laundry were done clearly everyday, my neatness was incomparable, but here someone asked me if I stain.

Have heard harsh words back at home, lived with snide remarks and this was just a bonus remark. Staring at my roommate, which probably hasn't talked more than two sentence, the hostility was indeed clear. From her brief forced introduction, heard her name is Anastasia, the strong dislike towards our arrangement, were clearly expressed on her features.

Till the extent, she made a call to her caretakers, to get her a new room, her words, were exactly, she feels uncomfortable staying with a personality like me, that my color was scaring her, and she never bothered how I felt hearing those words. Could see her peaceful face, the urge to abandon her and go for the event, tortured me, but I couldn't give in to my inner demons.

Anastasia! Ana, wake up, could see her irritated glance, her drowsiness reflecting on her Iris, on hearing her words, my heart taunted me for not following it's advice. "excuse me, don't call my initials again, we aren't close, and no chirpy discussions stay off my boundaries and lane" wow that was really hurtful said to no one in particular, the room was too uncomfortable, restricting the airflow, the hostility from her rippled in the atmosphere,

Running a quick shower and doing a bit of laundry, dressed up for the orientation, opted for a tight fitting knee length gown, with a leather jacket and pair shoes to compliment it. Rushing out to Lisa and Roselle's room, could see her scurry away with light steps, to the lavatory, to get her self primped up for the event, what an ungrateful soul, clicked my tongue.

ignoring her presence, silently prayed, she gets a new company cause I couldn't cope with the hostility. Licia!!! A sudden call brought my consciousness back, licia it repeated once more, tilting my head towards the call direction, Roselle and Lisa stood at the corner, waving at me with smiles, causing my initial frustration dissipating, maybe life isn't totally unfair whispered to myself.

Hello, we all greeted In unison, Lisa's green eyes beamed with happiness, the sincerity beaming in their eyes, dissipated the doubt swirling around me, that it was for a negative purpose. Roselle hazel eyes glinted in excitement, her childlike features innocently radiating out. Common let's get going.

Do you know where to locate the hall, Lisa asked suddenly, making we all halt our steps, that's true heard of it but wasn't aware of the location, we have got to make enquires suggested to them, or maybe follow the multitude, shrugged at my idea.

………………

Carl's p.o.v.

Hey Luca, newbies of this year are quite beautiful, Derick voice could be heard, with an underlying excitement, yes but few are eye sores, gosh Martin could testify we saw one of the darkest kid ever in the planet, not over exaggerating you could ask matins you know. Listening to their squabble, couldn't help but sigh, the name is Carl, coming from families of counselors, had heard fair share of stories of teenage struggles and their words had taught me a lesson, that the world need to listen to. Being a proprietor once, it felt like a second chance to redeem myself.

The black beautiful angel, who was been spoken about put the beauty of Aphrodite to shame, her beautiful brown orbs attracted my attention first. Her beauty, one that was unexplained, her doll like face radiated innocence. She was indeed a rare art piece, painted on the purest canvas by the maker himself

Being the faculty health president, had a lot of responsibility situated on my shoulders, and had to endeavor that my juniors were well welcomed. Staring at the departing figure of the students, orientation day was kind of boring, sighed for the ninth time.

Felicia's p.o.v

Oh my gosh!!! Anastasia is your mate, Lisa exclaimed with a shock filled expression. Hush it down, you don't want people misinterpreting our intent, I got it licia, just surprised guess my encounter with her made me more stupefied, never knew she was that hostile. Don't let her words, deter your mood, she smiled at me, while Roselle nodded in affirmation.

Warmth found it way to my heart, on hearing her words, honesty laced in them. common let's find a good spot Roselle cheerful voice drew everyone's attention back to the crowd. Student chattering away, could be seen, others sited quietly in their comfort zone, music keeping most company while few exhibiting affluence and wealth, could see Anastasia moving in elegantly, eyes trailed behind her. Few, jealous of her beauty, some envious of her wealth, others in admiration of such elegance and boldness, could see few seniors, loitering around the premises, motives of tainting a beautiful flower were as clear as the day in their smirks.

A blonde girl, with Charming amethyst eyes, her petite figure never deterred her elegance, followed her behind while the chatted away, maybe I felt a bit jealous of her beauty, of their conversation, while am her mate, being a very dark girl and surrounded with mostly light skinned beautiful girls, won't say I didn't feel out of place. The blacks over here, were moderately dark and beautiful, wasn't regretting being black, but wished to be moderately dark.

The feeling of my mate, detesting me came back, staring back at my friends felt like a loser, which I really was, for ever thinking of so, felt like I was only accepted because, we all were less among the crowd. No one wants to mingle with us or associate themselves with a conversation. Roselle was indeed obese, shouldn't have ever thought of body shaming her, but my inner demons were out for it.

Staring at Lisa, she was the better one in the group apart from her weird behavior of staring down, when passing a group of people, avoiding eye contact during interactions. Her freckles contrasted her skin beautiful, but her carriage was really bad. Maybe I was really with losers, and because I was a loser like them, the welcomed me to their crew. My logic were faulty, jealousy slowly blinded my reasoning.

Honestly was a jerk to think this way, but anyways did so. The urge to be accepted as Anastasia friend, to parole with her became overwhelming threatening to turn me bitter towards my friends. Roselle cute face turned into an ugly duckling in my eyes, bitterness were slowly taking its throne in my heart.

Felt watched, titling my neck towards my instinct, my brown orbs held his grey ones, seeing that he was been caught, he smiled while gauging my reaction. Turning back so fast, could feel my heart flip and dance with joy, but uncertainty destroyed my moment of happiness, how can an Adonis (metaphor- Adonis- a godlike beauty) smile towards me, his intentions are really hidden and it isn't a nice one. Obviously I battled with trust issues and you can't blame me for that.

Locating a perfect spot to seat, we trio moved to settle in. The Adonis looking guy caught up with us, my heart did rejoice, but my brains were alert, why will he want to sit with losers like us, glanced at his side features briefly, clicked my tongue disapprovingly, he obviously had Ill intentions. Sitting close to me, his friendly demeanor, calmed the anxiety, lingering on the atmosphere. Anastasia and her elegant crew eyes fixated on us, Maybe was a bit happy for the attention, but conscious if it was genuine.

The Adonis stranger beside me, was an epitome of beauty. His gray eyes looked like lighting on a raining day. So enchanting, hello dear am Carl what's yours, an angelic voice that had a hint of muscularity but still soft to the ears paused my roller coaster thought for a moment.

. . . .,,,,,,,, ...

Carl's p.o.v.

Been staring at the trio for quite a while, really don't Know what allures me to them. The feeling of guilt, that I was once a bully, until dad started involving me in his counseling sessions. Learning of how tough lives of the victim were, made me change. Seeing them, gave me an urge to protect them, from a second me.

The dark goddess, looked troubled her eyes flickered between her friends and some group of beautiful girls, comparison were written on her eyeballs. An Expression I could easily foretell. Am Carl and you are, stared at them for an introduction.

Roselle, the plump girl, responded to my question, her face beaming with smiles. Staring at the dark beauty beside me, don't know if my presence makes her uncomfortable, call me Felicia her voice came out forced or strained, couldn't fathom.

Our nervous baby couldn't lift her face, the fidgeting movement of her hands, indicated her nervousness. Roselle gave her a light tap, for encouragement, urging her to speak, my old me would have blurted out snide remarks, staring at her, her vulnerability exposed before me, but the urge to exploit it wasn't there, rather it was filled with the urge to help.

. . . .,,,,,,,, ...

Lisa's p.o.v

Finally settling down, a very handsome guy sat beside us, couldn't really tell his features, but the first glance I stole from him, he was indeed an exquisite of beauty. Casting my gaze to the floor, could feel the stares on me, but the sudden awareness that I was been watched, made me crawl back into my shell, was so embarrassed but I couldn't help it. Roselle gave me a nudge at my arm, which left me no choice but before I could respond, Felicia beat me to it, her agitated face wasn't hidden, it was shown for everyone to see her displeasure.

Hope I won't lose my friends again, because of my nonsensical attitude, chided myself. Could see Carl nodding, but his face were all smiles, at Least he wasn't irritated by my attitude that's a nice start. The hall was flooded with student of different races all seated and chattering away.

Carl engaged in a conversation with us, but licia never gave us a chance to speak, she kept responding words meant for us to him, like we were totally invisible. Guess Anastasia really made her cranky.

Lisa…. Roselle whispered towards me, turning towards her to give her my abrupt attention, I guess licia is in love with him and she thinks we will snatch her honey pot away from her, she chuckled lightly

Well couldn't disagree with her words, logically it made sense, Carl was indeed a honey pot, but the feeling of uncertainty gnawed at me, little facts or probably hint, were been left by her, her displeasure on little things, her subconscious attitude, indicated a wall, built against us. Maybe am overthinking or probably delusive to think such way, but being the kid in the shadow, people's reaction and actions were always visible to my keen eyes.

Couldn't disclose my thoughts to Roselle, I might have over exaggerated everything, bringing a rift among us, wasn't sitting well with me, could obviously be wrong.

"Dear student of Avac medical college, you all welcomed…………." a man with wired glasses, with a height below average, his protruded stomach showing no mercy to the buttons, which were in the verge of popping off, gave him a volleyball shape, spoke from the podium. Speech upon speeches were given. Rules and guild line all student must adhere to were uttered by Carl.

Never knew he was the health president, And like the dawn break the dusk came by. Carl had really become acquainted to us, attracting jealous stares from the onlookers. His words kept ringing in my brains, few minutes before we all departed to our various rooms. My hands were dragged back, before I could step into mine, started at him questioningly, my eyes demanding an explanation, his words made my smiles to stay and the warmth of my cheeks visible.

His words were exactly this " Lisa I just want to let you know, that you are very beautiful, so when you speak to me, want to see those beautiful green orbs staring at me, want to see those gorgeous freckles glittering beneath my eyes, so never look down when you are with me.

The redness on my cheeks Indicated how affected I was, no opposite gender had told me that I was beautiful, apart from Uncle Gary and uncle Sebastian. Roselle had nagged me to the point of hell abyss, to let her know what's making me blush and smile sheepishly. But I couldn't bring myself to say it.

Calling it a day, turned towards Roselle, what do you think college life has installed for us, it hasn't been so bad, although the snake like eyes of the seniors, trailing towards us when we were with Carl, made me question if the incoming days will be as peaceful as this. Honestly if Carl is a blessing or tragedy I couldn't tell, but time will unravel.

A quote that mother always say, flashed in my thoughts, everything that happened is fated to. Our destiny's been written and kept, trust me mom's belief could drive you nuts. I don't believe that, I beg to disagree, our destiny are made in our hands, the choices we make, are our responsibility, likewise the outcome, whatsoever results it bores, shouldering it, is our utmost responsibility.

Roselle drowsy eyes stared at me, and she Made a Statement which was indeed what college had for us. Her words were exactly Lili dear I think what college has for us is just lessons".

It really was indeed lessons, it taught things in harsh way, some in a pleasant manner, summoning it all up it was indeed lessons.

Dear diary is Lisa Esteban once again, survived another day good night.. Turning towards my right, switched off the lamp beside my   bed   stand.

Four

Choices determine allot.

Turn down that alarm!!! I shouted at frustrated, wake up sleepy head Roselle dragged me up, common on what's so important, a little bit of sleep wont hurt, could vouch is still the early hours of morning. Silly take a peep at the clock, her voice made me grunt out again, but it still piqued my curiosity, turning lazily, my eyelashes fluttered sluggishly.

Holy God!!!!!!!!! What the hell!!! Staring at Roselle rounded eye, mouth open, complementing it will my obstinate curls, looked like what you will describe a deranged woman.

Why didn't you drag me up soon, is noon already like how possible could that be, paced around anxiously, being so perplexed with the ordeal, fidgeted with my hands, the blames were all on Roselle, she could have beaten up, till drowsiness cleared my eyes. Her sudden outburst of laughter halted my movement, with her display, my brain cells kicked in, hastening my feet towards the window, stared out and everywhere was a bit foggy ....

I will murder you, launched at her, she really gave me a fright, her laughter caressed the walls of the room, sure who ever the alarm wasn't able to wake, with the noises and scream, should be fully conscious now.

Calm down.... Her laughter were in point of choking her, my tickles were punishment to her, God, could still feel the intense beating of my heart, due to the fright. What happened to the clock, asked her grudgingly, well a little prank wouldn't hurt, her cheerful smiles lightened up my mood. You started it, reminded her and my comeback will be worst, smirked devilishly.

Getting up dusted the invisible dust, on my sleeves. What an annoying way to see the sunrise. Get ready and let's mingle, a question flashed in my mind, it been tugging me for a while, I already knew the answer but just wanted her own view, Roselle do you think, am weird, stared at her curiously, like all answers lies on her tongue, maybe not over exaggerating stuff, but it kind of lies there.

............,,,,,,,.............

Roselle's p.o.v

An hour ago,

Staring at the clock, the indication 1:30 pm, fear gripped my heart, could have let my screams known, but in a second thought, took my phone to check if the alarm beep was off, the time there, washed away my visible worries, it was still 4:00 am, sighing tiredly, turned towards Lisa, her peaceful and smiling face indicating she was in a beautiful wonderland.

Tossing and turning, boredom slowly crept in, almost giving up to the calls of loneliness, an idea ignited in my brain like a light bulb. Nature in support of my plans, the alarm beeped, indicating it was already 5:00 am….

Placing the clock, directly on her ear, the reaction which I was expecting, came immediately, but still her eyes were still closed, and her voice husky due to lack of water, look at the clock sleepy head, her curiosity made her open her eyes, due to the intrusion to her sleep made her do it grudgingly

I thought she could handle the shock well, but unfortunately my assumptions were wrong, the scene was so hilarious, that tears seemed to accompany my laughter.

Minutes of Chase and smiles passed, her sullen face turned into smiles. Getting ready for the day, Li question halted, whatever movement I was engaging in. Opted to call her Li cause it seemed more close, Moreover she calls me rose and Felicia had a nickname too. Lili was anything from being weird. Her personality and heart couldn't be found in a goldmine.

Noticed she was socially impaired, maybe an introvert, we all are socially impaired, although hers came out a bit strong, but it could be worked on, that's what we were meant for, as her friend. Honestly without Li, might not be able to pull out my friendliness, her being beside me, accepting me for who I am. Boosted my confidence. The fact she couldn't freely talk to others, made me feel the responsibility, to speak to others for her sake.

Li you are far From being weird, you are amazing responded to her sincerely, most times what we need is just the compliment, you are beautiful, am proud of you, to keep us throughout the day.

Insecurities, one of the biggest factor that leads many to a depressing mode, was once in it's shackles, maybe haven't liberated myself from it, but the fact that I have one real friend beside me, could pull through.

Felicia's p.o.v

Anastasia! It's morning already, feeling torn, her reactions while touching her might come off too strong, just to be in the safer side, turned down the motion, of tapping her, moreover her statement on orientation day were still fresh.

Her eyes opened lazily, what's it so early her voice sounded so strain, the light rays in the skies, creeping through the spaces in which it's freedom was granted easily, adorned her features. She really was indeed beautiful like the goddess of beauty.

If only we could see the glimpse of how the future will be, perhaps a few stupid errors would have been avoided. It was just an ordinary can I talk to you, made me lose valuable companions, made me lose myself. Assuming you have somebody that thinks profoundly about you, a friend in time of trials and storm, never push them away, because you have seen friends of caliber and wealth.

It really might be a hazardous decision, but I was willing to take the tedious path. The discussion went on, as my mind has already orchestrated it, calling my friends lame, just to be in her trail of friends, telling her with her my college life will be blissful.

Maybe she saw me as pathetic wreck, cause that's what I was, kissed her shoes and threw my dignity, for affluence. Conditions were given to me, to follow her, I need to abandon others, turn a blind eye to whatever happens.

Questions about what, Carl had to do with us, was raised, guess she suppressed herself from asking the question earlier, due to her egoistical nature. Smelled jealous in the air, maybe my brains would have told me, we were all exceptional, that's why we got the opportunity to be chosen among the crowd, But what if we looked pitiful, like Ana presented it, he wanted to do it as a form of charity. Getting up, released an exhausted sigh. It's first day in class, we get to Know what classes and student, will be involved in our daily life.

Stared once again at Anna, how will I ignore Lisa and Roselle, way to go Felicia. Took a black boyfriend jeans(a slouchy, relaxed fit), with an orange free top, with bold writings of, black is beautiful, mum got the top on my eighteenth birthday. A pair of sneakers to compliment the look, entering the lavatory, choose to make due of a sluggish shower, there was much time actually.

……,……,………

Lisa's p.o.v

Wow can you feel it, the breath of freedom, rose demonstrated weirdly, which made me burst out into smiles, she was really a breath of fresh air, here I was apprehensive and restless, thankful for the first level student, generally all courses are somewhat, widespread at this point. During our second year we might take up different courses, I don't know how I will adapt with the pressure of not being with her.

Heading to Licia's block, so we trio could match out as usual. Li, rose voice interrupted my thoughts, turning towards what made her call for my attention, my eyes broadened in surprise. Wow! Licia has made up with her mate, then we are four members, guess the f4 teased rose lightly.

Her smiles widening more, honestly if cheeks could talk, they will moan in torment. Hi licia! Roselle raised her voice a bit in excitement, prompting to unwanted stares, chided rose in my mind, she's really was a full package of drama, see you are dumping me, teased her once again, while she rolled her eyes in response.

But the unexpected happen, how do people change, I questioned myself, some say the climate corrupts them, others say is company, thoroughly don't contradict their perspectives and fact. But in most cases people don't change due to those variables, they do on grounds that the need to, no factor influencing them.

Licia wasn't this person, was this her real self, were we played or too naive not to notice, glancing towards rose, our eyes conveyed, and it said one language, will she likewise betray me. No rose won't do such, licia showed signs, hints so obvious but we neglected it.

Few minutes ago….

Hi licia!, Rose excited voice called onto her, however her replied made us really dumbfounded. " Excuse me, we aren't friends nor close, don't appreciate strangers acting so close." Her retreating back with Anastasia sneer, were all we could see.

The sassy comment and laugh, made it more worst, she humiliated us in front of everyone, this wasn't alright, how could she do such. Could see Carl silhouette leaving, was he also disappointed in us. Anyways rose presence is sufficient.

Pathetic, Ana minion fueled the already intense atmosphere, deliberately making her voice sounds so audible, she spewed harsh words, " how desperate could some individuals be, acting so shameless" could feel the stares again, Roselle anger clearly displayed on her beautiful features.

Rose let's go, urged her to leave the suffocating atmosphere, I couldn't stand the stares and attention, might have an anxiety panic, which would kill my college life and courage.

How could licia, act so impudent and unfriendly, what went wrong!! Roselle voice increased gradually, she really was about to indulge in a fight. People change, had a go at dousing the flames, in as much I want to voice out my detest for licia conduct, my feelings of trepidation were more greater, Roselle only needs a spark to rain ruins, and my words might fuel it, if not careful.

The only thing I prayed for, was no bullies, couldn't Stand bunch of students Making my college life unbearable. High school were already enough tales, what a perfect day to start first class, sarcasm laced in my words, making rose scoff in annoyance.

Rose don't let it get to you, coaxed her to change her countenance, which really looked sour.

Common let's find a good spot, hooked my arm together with her, while dragging her to the middle row. After an hour or so, everyone settled down, while waiting for the supposed professor. Utilizing the time, scanned every one's faces, a really short looking boy, squeezed himself to the wall.

No offense, but he truly was so short, could see the stares and Snickers of others towards him, it really wasn't his fault brought forth like that. No need of making things unbearable for him, muttered inaudibly, three seats away from us, two guys, with indistinguishable features were seated, undoubtedly they were twins, but what made them stood out, was the unusual paleness of skin. Assuming vampires were genuine, and not mythical that's a reasonable illustrations of what was written on the novel books.

Their skin so white and pale, cheeks tainted with red blushes. They looked like rare species, blonde and white strands of hair embellished their features. It all screamed royalty, I don't know but the fact they were oblivious to the stares, and tattles added to their uniqueness.

Few whispers made way to my hearing, oh my gosh is the height real, damn she really put the world tallest man to shame, jeez how's the view up there. Turning my eyes towards the direction of the whispers, my eyes extended in shock, how possible is that height, tapped Roselle, which was left astonished.

Five

New fellow

Vanessa's p.o.v

Mum dropped me off, with beaming smiles, go on Nessa, you are already late. Stared at mum for the hundredth time, gathered my composure, stepped out of the car bravely. Could see the shocked and stunned filled faces of everyone, was use to the gaze, but I couldn't help but feel so scared .

Hi family I go by Vanessa crox, my height could be considered a 10.9 feet tall. Oh yeah I know you are stunned, what could I do, couldn't help my growth, maybe it was my folks hereditary shortcomings, maybe it was a genetic disorder, however I was unable to mind pretty much.

Been tormented, been body shamed, the world mentality was debilitated, well wrapped up seeing a specialist last month, was a suicidal and depressed patient, months passed before I could finally acknowledge my trepidation, yet it changed nothing. Truly was alright with the shocked appearances, it truly was okay.

37

However I wasn't okay with the hurtful remark, wasn't okay been tormented, been called names. Tracking down the lecture hall, took in full breath before letting my presence known, everyone stared at me like I was some kind of alien, some like I was an amusement in their eyes. Either way it was unnerving.

Stepping into the hall, the murmurs got louder and stronger, couldn't find a spot to seat, sighting an unfilled seat next to a black beautiful girl, with a tee engraved black is beautiful, it indeed was, beside her an elegant aristocrat beauty was seated, anyways moved towards that direction but before I could seat, the elegant beauty disrupted my movement.

"Sorry but not sorry, but this seat isn't for lame people, so go find another one, causing everyone to burst out in laughter. Could feel my heart clenching in anger and shame. However before I could dare to move, a sweet voice hindered it, her voice blended with roughness and delicacy.

"And you doll faces, never knew you carried a seat to school" she jeered and passed me, moving to sit at the seat roll before it. Could see the scrunched up face of my oppressor. Served her right, stared at my hero, her oversized jumper and tee, gave her a boyish look. Her hair dyed with the sunset color, her blue eyes gazed at me back, making me flinch.

Hey you, she called out, you want to stare at me all day, get you a** seated. You obstructing the air, yet her words never came out discourteous, rather it came out amicable. Situated adjacent to her, decided to introduce myself. Am Nessa, hi for what you did earlier.

She scoffed and stared directly at me, you know what I disdain, pompous whelps, manner less kids, and someone that can't stand up or express anything for themselves. Weaklings, totally disdain that, and you know you fall under the last classification, so no need to express gratitude.

Although her words stung like a honey bee, but I really was defenseless, right now I couldn't still retaliate back with words. Staring at her nothing seemed to unfazed her, her nonchalant disposition intrigued me. But life made it fair for her, she wasn't the one been asked how's the view up there. She was the hero not the victim, not the one at the end rope of receiving derogatory speeches.

Scanning around, could feel the intense stare come from my side, tilting my neck towards the ominous feeling, four seat away from me, two student stared at me in awe, are my eyes playing tricks on me, clearly what I saw in those eyes weren't scorns but rather fascination.

Held their gaze, studying their features, the fat looking girl had a cheerful and blinding smile complimenting her childlike features while the other had a wild beauty. Her messy curls rolled freely up. Lose strands escaping and flowing freely with the wind. Her green eyes like the lush grass.

She indeed was beautiful, returning back their friendly smiles, won't hurt to be polite. The lecture went on expected, allot of student names were known, it really wasn't so bad. Getting up and facing everyone eyes again tugged me, decided to seat and be the last to move, might be a silly suggestion but definitely sticking to it.

The most handsome guy here stared at me before leaving the premises, well I couldn't say he was the most good looking kid in the hall. The attention twins were really charmers, but he had features of your dream fantasy boy.

Won't you leave too, someone beckoned to me, oh it was those two individuals earlier. What lame excuse should I give, we have one more lecture remaining. Few hours from now, won't just be seated till then, battling with what excuse to bring up. Her voice sounded again, well if you don't mind you could join us to the canteen, the name is Roselle what's yours.

Of course I didn't mind but what of them don't they mind walking with a specie like the world has painted it to be. Picking up my stuff, followed behind, my name is Vanessa crox, gave a light introduction while staring down at them and them looking up to me.

Is Lisa.. Lisa Esteban the wild beauty spoke this time, her face pointed towards the floor, but in some cases she raises it to meet me on an eye level. Guess she's the shy type.

Six

Pain

Lisa's p.o.v

Its been three weeks Now, allot has happened and allot more will happen. Met student and individuals that Life had explain the actual meaning of unfairness, I thought life had it messed up for me but not really, others were literally going through hell.

Don't misquote me, it wasn't all about the negativity, allot of positivism too, met amazing friends, the memories, the smiles, guess what been wooed by the hottest guy in school, although rosy keeps telling me his hiding me from the world.

Probably, Carl don't really acknowledge me in front of his friends, he treats me like a random stranger, overhead when a senior asked him, to define our relationship, his words were exactly she's just my junior am looking out for them, confronted him, due to the rose's threat, she vowed to do it, if I her words were neglected.

But his reply was just vague, he didn't want unnecessary attention to me, still a newbie and let's just give things time. Took in his words with reasoning and understanding.

Did I mention a guy named lex been after Roselle, although he gives me the creeps, told Roselle about it but she lashed out on me, I guess I did overstep my boundaries. Honestly lex gives me a vibe that his just toying with Roselle. I really hope he isn't doing such, couldn't shake off the weird feelings.

Vanessa had become so close to us, that we literally became inseparable, although the nasty remarks about her height weren't really subdued. Turning a blind eye to it is her specialty, she's really doing better.

Donald was the name of the super short guy, he really was heavily bullied, unfortunately he dropped out two days ago, the comments really were getting to him, couldn't blame him. Told Carl to try going to his place and maybe coax him in returning back to school as the school president.

Honestly his reply was vague. Well another guy took over his place, he had this excessive sebum, on his face making him prone to acne. His been battling with acne since he really was a kid. Making his face look a bit rough, due to the excessive acne and black heads on his face.

His been called an ape, different kinds of ugly name. Some say his too disgusting to be seen. His life was really a leaving hell, would have suggested reporting to the counselors, but at the end nothing will be accomplished. Roselle had actually suffered from nasty remarks like names like elephant. She actually eats less, than any of us, however her fatness were genetic. Days came by, were consolation was all I could offer. Permitting her to rest on my arms to the next morning.

Could go on and on, about countless things i noticed, licia had really become a total person, her transformation wasn't so great, felt like she was rather a captive to Anastasia and her lackey's, she did all the errand, just to parole with them, So nauseating.

Anastasia generally Converses with Carl, since she turned into the president of our Dept, assisted by the twins. Carl never feels ashamed with her, they rather acts like couples. Some days I can't help but feel so envious of my boyfriend.

All around been attempting to deal with my insecurities and strategies to be sociable. Had to read tons of book and advises on ways of breaking this bondage, But I kind of love the book written by counselor Harriet Williams, "Enough of being mute". Honestly the most amazing part of the book, was the point at which the writer presented a rule that helped her, tackle her shyness and that's "whatever happens should happen". kept those words buried in my heart.

Totally find it aiding, in my utterances, I recite and chant those words, for braveness, it gives me the courage to speak. The fact they I won't be killed by tormentor, my apprehensions were meaningless. As easy it might sound it isn't easy.

Sitting alone for minutes, been waiting for that charming being, Roselle. Her boyfriend called her, in terms of wanting to make things official or stuff. You wondering why I wasn't with her, had an argument with her about her boyfriend. He thoroughly gives the creepy vibe.

Noticing the mumbles and noises, what's going on asked no one in particular, everyone was watching something on their phones and running towards a specific direction. My eyes flickered dubiously.

The air became a bit suffocating, indicating something bad was happening, my feet hastened towards the direction, everyone was dashing to. Lisa! Lisa!, Nessa voice could be heard behind me, causing my steps to halt. Glancing at her briefly, could see her panicking and shocked Expression..

With rushed pants and gasp, you have got to watch this, urging me to stare at the phone on her palms. My attention shifted from her disheveled face, due to sweat and stared at the phone, behold Roselle was been shamed and ridiculed by lex, licia was his girlfriend She sat comfortable beside him, like an evil demoness, beside his devilish ruler.

Roselle broken eyes, indicated how profound the scar was, if he wasn't interested, why lead her on and act like a douche bag. Sudden rage came upon me, rage about the system, cause she was obese, doesn't mean her emotions were turned off. The onlookers were same with her tormentor, the soft tears gliding down on her delicate cheek, were seen by them, but no one decided to step out, no one said this wrong.

Whatever will happen let it happen, chanted it to my brain for courage, staring at Nessa with a resolved look, I have a best friend to defend, stormed out after uttering my words, From hastened feet, it turned into a run, not minding the words spoken, dashed towards the scene.

There she was, with a tear stained face, encompassed by selfish jerks. Squeezing myself in, approached her tenderly, her eyes bore into mine with one fathomable message, you were right about him. But this wasn't the time to put blames, or justify myself. It was the time to depart that suffocating atmosphere.

Turning towards lex, chanted the phrase once again. Haven't seen such a douchebag like you, my voice visibly shaken in rage, courage which I never exhibited in my life surged out. You are a double crossing cheater. Do everyone know how you, called her the most beautiful girl, that no girl tops her place in your heart.

Does your leach of a girlfriend Know, how long you wooed her and begged for her attention. You are so sick, staring at licia, couldn't resist the urge to shake my head, you life is too pitiful, and is worst that a dark goddess like you, ended with a thrash like him.

Could see the bewildered faces of everyone, Roselle wasn't an exemption, it was clearly outlined in her features, that my actions were unexpected. Who would have expected the kid with the top notch, insecurities and weirdness, be so outspoken. Bravo Lisa, smiled within me.

Dragging Roselle, out of their presence, it felt like I was a legend. My braveness would have had a beautiful ending if not for the last phrase, spoken out of lex, causing my knees to tremble. Staring at Carl, he too was stunned by the phrase, could see Anastasia mocking face.

Nessa had to drag we both out of there, which I appreciated because, we were too broken. For what reasons, muttered to myself why were we picked on, cause we weren't like them, my sub consciousness replied to my perplexed mind. That's the world we were brought into.

Won't let it break me, whispered to myself. Counselor Harriet made a quote. *Confront those mountains, to set yourself liberated". That's exactly what I will do, untangling myself from rosy and Nessa gasp, moved back to where the ordeal, took place, could see the dispersing figure, due to the show was over.

Don't they feel repulsed, glared harshly to the eyes that might mine. Honestly can't believe am pulling this. Like where the sudden courage, I guess reading books concerning my problems helped step out a bit. Locating my target, Carl was seen arguing with lex, keeping my gaze at him, trudged towards him, could see the anxious look on his features.

Giving him no time to understand his predicament, dragged him out, towards a nearby locker. Speak, if you have anything to say, am giving you the chance to, bravo can't imagine that I didn't stutter, the rage boiling In me, were clearly reflected in those green beautiful orbs of mine.

Could see his anxious and guilty stricken face, chuckling darkly, whispered to the air, so is true. I thought you were decent, never knew you were more than an asshole.

Toying with us is quite hilarious right, could see him want to utter flimsy excuses, to get himself out of the spider web. But the words never escaped his mouth. What now, the cat bit u tongued, scoffed at him.

The nerve of you, pretending to be a saint, those craps you said about coming from a prestige family of counselors. I can't even hate you, cause is not worth my emotions. Lisa he called onto me, his voice at the verge of breaking, but I couldn't feel remorseful, it could be an act. Cocking up my eyebrows, stared at him impatiently, am deeply sorry he blurted out. Hey dude, sorry doesn't fix a broken plate, you toying with my emotions and shattering my heart.

You think is a football pitch, where you go to kick ball, is a damn breathing heart, he said I was your experiment, you were using me due to a sickening bet. Your professes of love were just a joke, thanks for breaking me and making me strong.

. . . . ,,,,,,, ...

Vanessa's p.o.v

Couldn't stand this anymore, staring at Roselle, her brokenness reflected on her features, lex was of no good, I knew it. Been insulted regularly, received snarky remarks, been asked if I was a giraffe mutant. Fought back, but it got me into detention. How dare they ask me if I was a giraffe mutant. Everyday I pass by, been asked how's the sky view, been called giant.

It's sickening, honestly thought of ending my life over and over again, bugged me. Who will love a giant like me, no one would want me. My parents loved me but could see their ashamed gazes. Being suicidal and depressed, was on the verge of falling into a dark abyss, the only thing keeping my sanity were Roselle and Lisa.

Been called the lame group, but still they were my only light in the tunnel. Staring at Roselle, yes she was fat maybe a little more than average. Maybe a bit obese, that doesn't mean she doesn't feel emotions.

Asshole, if he didn't want her why lead her on, just to slander her in public. I thought Carl was a bit decent but all this was just a game

47

to them. As the clock tick , my anxiousness increased, Lisa isn't back. Honestly was so dumbfounded, when she challenged lex. Her features given her exuberance of a warrior. Watching her break after lex words shattered me. Minutes turned to hours, Roselle gently drifted to Dreamland, Lisa was no where to be found.

Making sure Roselle was properly situated, went in search of Lisa, unfortunately my eyes met Carl first. Although Carl had been friends with Roselle and Lisa, we really aren't In talking mode, he either avoids me, or respond curtly to my talks.

Dusk was few minutes away, the beautiful sky had let out it exotic orange paint, the sun had hidden itself. Excuse me, where's Lisa? Asked him skeptically. Honestly he really was the last person in my mind to ask for Lisa.

I don't know, she left hours ago, is she missing, stared at him irritated, now you care right, glared furiously at him, all this was his damn fault. Passing by, heard whispers of a weird girl, playing basketball ball alone.

Rushing towards the court, Lisa was sprawled on the floor, could see sweat glinting underneath the light. Lisa! Dashed towards her, causing her to shift her attention towards me, are you okay, been so worried.

She smiled crazily, like a psychotic person, "enough of being mute" her words repeated countless times like a broken record.

Lisa p.o.v.

After the insane ordeal, headed towards the b-ball court to let go off some steams. Sitting there, could feel my nerves settle a bit. Feeling a presence close to me, tilted my neck towards the fellow. The pimple face guy, glanced at him for seconds, smiled in acknowledgment. We both sat there for hours, no one uttering anything.

The silence would have been unnerving, but my psyche being occupied with it's drama, couldn't care. Am envious of you his voice broke the silence, well my cerebrum had to reset to make sure, the words it was processing was deemed precise.

Excuse me you are what??, Couldn't help but blurt out my thoughts, are you perhaps mocking me, due to the circumstances, stared intensely at him for answers, my green eyes, mirroring the secret fury, subdued within it.

Nothing like that, he responded quickly, urging him with my eyes to continue, my last stand of patient were letting loose. Am envious of you, he repeated once more, of course I heard him earlier on, wasn't either daft or deaf.

Why asked him inquisitively, observing myself, nothing so spectacular worth admiring, noticing my actions, he let out a brief chuckle, but his eyes held sadness. Honestly I wish I could stand for myself like you did, watched the video, lex did a nasty thing, but the astonishing part was that you stood firm and retaliated courageously.

Am envious that you could do it. Here I am, wallowing in self pity, suicidal thought, I really wish I had a voice to speak out like you did. His words snapped me back to the harsh reality. I had no voice, sincerely am flabbergasted with my own revelation, am no wonder woman, simply a wrecked lady that her constraint of anguish broke.

Stared at him, i felt like I found a purpose, yes a voice not really that the torment will end, but let the voice be loud and clear, the welcome night party blurted out, causing him to be perplexed. Smiled brightly at him, thanks allot.

The name is Lisa what's yours, he responded back gently, you are trending everyone knows your existence. Mine is Andrew, his response made me understand the force a video could be.

Watching his retreated steps, decided to rest on the floor to initiate a great plan. Time isn't a leisure for me. Lisa!! A sudden call, dragged my eyes towards the yelling. Oh nessa, her concerned gaze, tugged my heart. Made them worry, never knew how time flies, enough of being mute, spoke the first sentence that my brain formulated.

Seven

Voice out

Y ou are getting the hang of it girl, Mel whistled, days upon days, turned to weeks upon weeks of practice. Stood at the platform once again, and gave my presentation, never gave out the content of my speech, it was an unexpected package, meant to be unwrapped in due date.

With the welcome night party moving toward rapidly, just two days ahead, rehearsed on my anxiety in front of large audiences, at long last could remain on the stage, without having a mental breakdown. After the crazy ordeal, an idea formulated, to voice out my agony loud and clear.

Could say am now a VIP, not in the great way, but honestly my life been publicized, my practices been posted in the school forum, everyone is aware that a speech will be spoken by me. Have allot of people anticipating in my speech, in which am not in any event

51

anticipating them, although is actually a great turn out, need the numerous to hear my voice.

After the incident, examined everything with Roselle and my plans, in which she gave me her full support, needed to run recordings on student, experiencing from Same trials, same psychological mistreatment and all has been recorded and organized in the flash drive.

Classes been chaotic, yet fun. Nessa had a suicide endeavor, which fueled my anger. Her moniker was genetic disorder, which was cruel, no one minds rather, everyone hears the nasty remarks, still disregards it, and Most indulge in making her life miserable.

Roselle, Nessa and I ended in detention, few days ago, I didn't actually take in the fight, just the peacemaker, but we all were punished. Least I forget, Carl and I are presently in the talking mode, I know you probably contemplating whether am insane, to converse with him or stuff.

Well his the president and obviously in my arrangement one way or another he will be involved, however trust me he truly feels remorseful of his actions. A week ago he gave me a book he was dealing with, despite the fact it hasn't been named and presently i comprehend his perspectives aren't far fetched from mine.

· · · · · ·,,,,,,,· · · · · · · · · · · ·

The welcoming night

Gosh you look astonishing, wasn't over exaggerating but Roselle looked amazing, she had on her body, a strapless sliver gown, which wrapped her curves perfectly, the good thing about her stature, was she didn't have a stomach fat, it kind of was astounding. Her black silvery bag complimented it, paired with matching black silvery lined heels.

Her cheerful smiles graced her lips, before I could comprehend my situation was already in a bone crushing embrace. Nessa stepped in a minute after, seeing the emotional tension, she joined in too. I can't breath girls, I muffled out my words with great difficulty.

So sorry, they both chuckled, oh my God is that Ness, rosy words brought my attention to Nessa, she looked beautiful, she generally been delightful, yet she looked extra. Her two piece pants and shirt did equity to her looks. Elegance oozed out like streams.

Well you look beautiful as always, they both Smiled at me, gracious I overlooked my existence. Couldn't resist the opportunity to concur, needed to request mum to order an enchanting gown. And she delivered. Putting on a sleeveless outfit with a fabric free back. Body fitted, with a long slit in the front, a white fabric lined with golden sparkles it truly was indeed enchanting.

Matched it with a brilliant heels, a tad of cosmetics to accentuate my eyes, and lips, my messy curls were braided a bit in the front, the rest were let loose. Am proud of myself no longer the self hate.

Let's go, we all yelled together, you are crazy mumbled loudly, causing everyone to burst out in laughter.

The buzzing sound of music and the chattering of students graced my eyes. It truly was an awesome party, everywhere was crowded, could see most seniors seated and munching on their foods. The time is here, glancing back to the crowd, could say the multitude exceeded my assumptions My nervousness were clearly paving it's way to me, clutching onto my dress. Could hear the mic clearing sound, indicating the party is really about to start, Carl stood on the stage, his Caucasian color Popping underneath the light, blue truly was the perfect color for him, those blue babies hugged his body flawlessly, could see the look of admiration and lust on the onlookers face.

Licia and Anastasia together with their minions, were standing a little meters away from us, well they generally been beautiful and tonight the looked perfect. Held licia gaze for a moment, her eyes conveyed sadness and words, the nervousness threatening to overwhelm me dissipated, I need to be a voice, for individuals like licia I need to speak out.

Tightening my resolve again, whatever want to happen should happen, enough of the shell. Gazed at the platform once again with fierceness, am prepared to take on any mountain. Recounted my #1 phrase, you definitely understood what it is "whatever will happen should happen" smiled broadly, could see the weird Stare of Nessa and rose's statement Making me chuckle, she acts psychotic, ignore her she threw me a playful wink, which I responded with a chuckle.

Minutes turned to hours, speech upon speech were given and finally the long anticipated time was due, could see the assurance stare, from my companions and the enthusiastic gazes from everyone.

Everyone stared at me like, I was an alien could feel the anxiety returning, stared at Roselle and Nessa, their smiles gave me the strength, standing on the podium it felt like I held power, felt like everyone was beneath me.

Clearing my throat, the crowd disrupted with laughter, would have fidgeted or got annoyed but I calmly waited for it to subside a tad, are you done asked the crowd, which brought the deafening silence, you all know my name Lisa Esteban, if someone read a fortune of mine four months ago, and make a statement that one day I will stand, in front of you all, in front of this multitude and relay a speech would have beaten the hell out of the person.

But the system forced me, you all forced me to step out of my shell, to voice out the lump, the aggravation, the anguish we all face everyday forced my hands. Made Allot of recordings, which will be aired later, but let me show you few clips, Nessa video was projected and everyone watched her statement, you all Wondering what's all this about, couple minutes back you saw the clip.

You sent someone to kill her precious life, to end her own existence, and is regarded as an innocuous humor, words like genetic disorder, I surmise they were casual remarks, the giraffe mutant, that you always utter, guess it was all essential for an innocuous joke. How did we get to this point when our conscience never bothers us.

That guy over there, Andrew, am certain many doesn't know him by his initial, well I didn't if not weeks ago, we all know him as the pimple face guy, who cares assuming his emotions were crushed, terrible remarks were made, ape was rather associated with him, than his identity, he has been called disgusting, who made you the appointed judge,

How perfect are you, you bully him all the time to satisfy a rotten ego, why you all staring at me like am the villain here. You all know my words are truth, the body shaming of individuals.

She's obese and is nothing you should be concerned about, I call it joblessness to take one's predicament on your head. So what up in an event she's stout, aren't you worn out on the same taunting sentence, others think the heart is a play ground, you run your balls anyhow, not caring about the injuries and scars you inflicted.

Everyone has an issue or not, however it doesn't make you the judge, this my words to everyone here, you all beautiful, to all that have suffered psychological abuse, insecurities, trust me, was the queen of insecurity actually, you all are astounding, our highlight (features) are what makes us rare and distinct. Is the fact that we are not like everyone, never permit anyone step on your heart, suicide ought to never cross your heart, why give them satisfaction they opt for.

The pimples makes you unique, beauty is just the outward look, it incorporates the within as well. So what if it wasn't the perfect shape, live the best out of it, endeavor to be the better you and shove it to their faces they can't rather downgrade you, rather they make you stronger each day.

To everyone calling us the lame group, proudly sponsored by the lame group, much appreciated. I did it, whispered to myself, the reverberating applaud at the atmosphere brought a sensation of fulfillment. The smiles of my love ones, the elated faces of the professors and lecturers which I never knew were there, made me realize I did the right thing.

The tears flowing from Nessa face, but this time around it was the tears of fulfillment made me know I finally stepped out of my shell. To dedicate my voice to the world, allot of struggles were excluded, however the few I could am proud of it, I present to you my book, stepping out of your shell.

The   end.

Eight

Conclusion

Y ou there, you are beautiful, there words are their perspectives, adoring yourself first is all the matters, words get to you, when your hearts and mind are against yourself and when you have upheld their own untruths. Build the confidence, carry yourself like an esteemed valor you are, when it gets too much confront the mountains, don't always be accepting and quiet, enough of being mute, take action of progress.

I know perhaps it isn't the best figure sort out there, it isn't the best condition out there, that's why you need to love yourself and work for the best version of yourself, you didn't make you, so stop wallowing in self pity, suicide thought, why will you entertain the thought of ending it all, giving them the satisfaction that the want, when you can be the better you.

I comprehend is extreme, it gets rough and it gets excruciating, you feel overwhelmed, but that ought to make you stronger, much love   from   me.   .

Afterword

The pain that doesn't kill you, ought to make you stronger.